W9-CTB-105

The Sky's the Limit

Stories of *Discovery* by Women and *Girls*

Catherine Thimmesh   Illustrated by **Melissa Sweet**

HOUGHTON MIFFLIN COMPANY BOSTON

www.houghtonmifflinbooks.com

The text of this book is set in 12-point Fairfield.
The illustrations are mixed media.

Library of Congress Cataloging-in-Publication Data
Thimmesh, Catherine.
The sky's the limit / by Catherine Thimmesh ; illustrated by Melissa Sweet.
p.   cm.
Includes bibliographical references and index.
Summary: Presents brief accounts of the work of a variety of women and
girl discoverers in such fields as astronomy, biology, anthropology, and medicine.
RNF ISBN 0-618-07698-0   PAP ISBN 0-618-49489-8
1. Science—Miscellanea—Juvenile literature. [1. Women in science.
2. Science—Miscellanea.] I. Sweet, Melissa, ill. II. Title.
QB163.T478   2002
500'.82—dc21
2001039111

Printed in Singapore
TWP 10 9 8 7 6 5 4 3 2 1

Photo Credits
p. 10: photo courtesy of Dr. Vera Rubin and the Carnegie Institute of Washington's
    Department of Terrestrial Magnetism
p. 14: photo by Beverly White Spicer, courtesy of Denise Schmandt-Besserat
p. 20: photo by Katie Hargrove, courtesy of Donna Shirley
p. 25: photo by Hugo van Lawick/National Geographic Society, courtesy of Jane
    Goodall and the Jane Goodall Institute and the National Geographic Society
p. 32: photo by John Weinstein, courtesy of Sue Hendrickson and the Field Museum
p. 37: photo courtesy of Anna Sofaer and the Solstice Project
p. 41: photo courtesy of Bettmann Archive
p. 47: photo courtesy of June Moxon
p. 54: photo by Scholastic Photography, courtesy of Katie Murray
p. 58: photo courtesy of Eli Penberthy
p. 61: photo courtesy of Rachael Charles

For Mom and Dad,
who discovered the rewards of reading and
generously shared their discovery with me
—C. T.

To my nieces, Abbe, Jenny, and Claire,
who helped me discover new ways
to indulge my brother's children
—M. S.

Contents

Introduction

"I think, at a child's birth, if a mother could ask a fairy godmother to endow it with the most useful gift, that gift should be curiosity."
—Eleanor Roosevelt

Bang! And just like that, the universe popped into being. Curious, isn't it? How did it happen? *When* did it happen? What did it look like? What did it sound like? There was not a single witness to this most momentous event; so how can we ever hope to know the details of the universe's origins? And yet the moment of genesis—the actual birthday of the universe—may very well have been recently discovered by astronomer Wendy Freedman and her team of researchers.

Whether by a fairy godmother's gift or by less mystical means, women—from the dawn of time to the eve of today—have indeed been endowed with a healthy dose of curiosity. And their curiosity has led them to seek, to explore, to uncover, to probe with question after question, to dig up, to find out . . . to discover.

Co-leading a team of researchers, Wendy Freedman, with the aid of the Hubble space telescope, discovered (in the most accurate measure to date) the Holy Grail of astronomy—the age of the universe. To do this, she first had to determine how fast the universe is expanding—not an easy task. But over the course of six long years she succeeded in finding the elusive expansion rate, known as the Hubble constant. Next, to learn the age of the universe, Wendy had to add to her calculations the universe's known density (because density slows the rate of expansion). Finally, combining years of observations and complex calculations, Wendy Freedman and her team discovered the approximate age of the universe, arriving at a value of 13 (with an error margin of plus or minus 2). That's 13 *billion* years old!

Despite their scant recognition in the history books, century after century, decade after decade, year after year, and day after day, women have been responsible for some of the most astounding discoveries: the origins of writing and counting, pulsars, ancient tin mines, X and Y chromosomes . . . dinosaur bones. In 1744, Elizabeth Lucas Pinckney discovered the indigo plant in South Carolina (the natural source for blue dye). In 1847, from the roof of her house, Maria Mitchell discovered a comet. In 1946, Dorothy Crowfoot Hodgkin discovered the chemical structure of penicillin. And in the year 2000, Dr. Martina Berger and her team discovered a virus present in the spinal cords of people who have Lou Gehrig's disease (ALS), which may lead researchers to the cause of the debilitating disease.

Perhaps the most notable—certainly the best known—woman discoverer is Madame Marie Curie, the French physicist and radiation chemist who, in the late 1800s, discovered the elements radium and polonium and introduced the concept of radioactivity to the world. She was the first woman to win the prestigious Nobel Prize and one of the few people to receive two Nobels. She died of leukemia, brought on by long-term exposure to radiation. But Marie Curie's discoveries live on—as did the path she blazed for future women scientists and discoverers.

Discovery is itself multidimensional. A new find is a discovery; so too is an old find rediscovered by someone new. And if discovery, by definition, is diverse, so too are the women and girls—the discoverers—themselves: archeologists, biologists, cosmologists . . . zoologists. But the great part of discovery—the really fun part—is that you don't have to have an "-ist" in your job title to discover something. Discovery, in its simplest terms, requires a sense of awareness and the ability to distinguish the new and noteworthy. Discoveries happen in myriad ways. Some are purposefully sought, others are stumbled upon. Some are recognized immediately, others realized only after years of study. In some cases, a discovery's significance is elusive—perhaps needing future discoveries to explain it.

Today, women and girls in all walks of life are unleashing their curiosity and forging their own paths to discovery—paths that zigzag and weave about freely, unbound, unhindered, limitless; paths that will prove the sky's the limit for possibility and discovery. Upon reflection, it becomes clear that women's discoveries—past and present—have helped to define the very world in which we live. These stories are a celebration of their journeys.

Chapter One

lichen

dis-cov-er

/dis-'kev-er/ vb dis-cov-ered;
dis-cov-er-ing

1. to obtain knowledge of, as through observation or study

2. to be the first to find, learn of, or observe

Discovery may apply to something requiring exploration or investigation or to a chance encounter

Beatrix Potter
Lichens are both algae and fungi

Best known for her lovable rabbits—Flopsy, Mopsy, Cottontail, and Peter—Beatrix Potter was a renowned author and illustrator of numerous classic children's books. But her first love was natural history. From an early age she collected and painted plants, flowers, birds, and other animals. She was fascinated by the plants she drew and undertook an intense study of fungi, spending many hours at the nearby British Museum of Natural History studying them under a microscope and making detailed, scientifically accurate drawings. In 1896, through her studies, she discovered that a lichen consists of both an alga and a fungus—living interdependently, or separately, but as one. (Previously, a lichen was thought to be just an alga, with perhaps a fungus present only as a parasite.) She made accurate drawings of her finds, but the scientific community showed no interest. Disillusioned, she abandoned her scientific pursuits and took up illustrating. It would be many years before her discovery of the duality of lichens was finally accepted as fact. It is fun to note, though, that many of the paintings of plant life that adorn her famous books originally began as scientific renderings for a book on fungi that she was hoping someday to write.

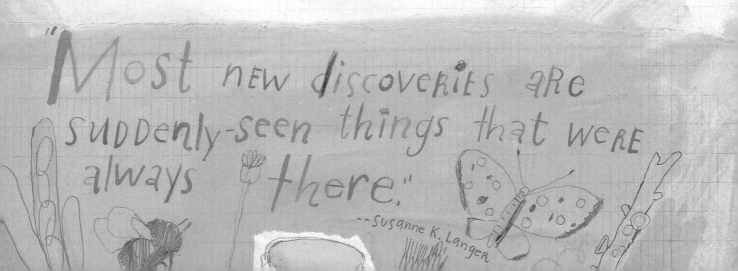

"Most new discoveries are suddenly-seen things that were always there."

--Susanne K. Langer

It Sure Is Dark Out There
Vera Rubin

As the stars spring to life in the evening sky, scientists and other curious people peer out into the vast deepness of the universe—home of countless brilliant, spinning galaxies; home of the beginnings of time. They look through their telescopes and actually see the UNIVERSE. Or do they?

When astronomer Vera Rubin found that 90 percent of the matter that makes up the universe is invisible to us, her discovery was completely unexpected. It was a discovery that, at first, was just too much for some to believe. She certainly didn't mean to initiate controversy. In fact, she had deliberately tried to avoid it. And yet, here she was, suggesting that what we see, and what we thought was the entire universe—including stars, galaxies, and gaseous clouds—was really only a minute fraction of the universe, only about 10 percent. In other words, 90 percent of the universe actually couldn't be seen. Scientists dubbed the invisible part "dark matter."

"From the earliest of times, astronomers thought the galaxy consisted of exactly what you saw," Vera said. *"They thought that these dark regions were just regions that didn't have anything in them."*

Vera became hooked on stars at an early age, building her first telescope at fourteen. Although she categorized it as "crummy" (it was an old linoleum tube with a small lens), she *was* able to see through it. And so began her lifelong pursuit of astronomy. She was thrilled with the beauty of the skies, spurred by an unwavering curiosity about how the universe works.

In the late 1970s, while working at the Carnegie Institution's Department of Terrestrial Magnetism, Vera developed a study to investigate the dynamics of spiral galaxies, hoping to learn more about their evolution and formation. Many people had studied the centers of galaxies—those densely packed areas of luminosity, or brightness—but no one had paid any serious attention to their outer edges.

During the developing phase, Vera actually had her own two-minute song. She timed herself singing "In the Still of the Night" ("Shoo-doo, shooby do . . .") for exactly two minutes, and she would sing that song each developing phase . . . just in case. When you're cold and exhausted, she said, you never know when you might forget to start the timer.

"I wasn't looking to discover something," explained Vera. "I just wanted to learn about the outsides of galaxies. I had always been interested in how galaxies ended—just because it was completely unknown. So to do that I was studying how stars orbit in a galaxy. [They all orbit around the center.] It had always been assumed that the stars farther and farther from the center would go slower and slower because the gravitational force would be less."

And that force would be less, it was thought, because there was less matter—less material. But that was not what Vera found. Her first significant observations were of the nearby galaxy Andromeda.

"I sat in the dome of the observatory," said Vera. "The dome is open to the air and always kept unheated—it has to be at outside air temperature or else the air will shimmer and give bad images. So I would spend the whole night in the cold, all bundled up."

At the end of the night—a twelve-hour stint during which she took two photographic exposures—there was the Big Decision: to go to sleep or to develop the film plates.

"It was a toss-up between going to sleep or doing them, but I was afraid of making a mistake. Much of the process is done in the dark and everything is timed," she said. "I had to put them in the developer for two minutes, and then wash them in water, and then put them into the next chemical and so on . . . Everything had to be done with a timer, and almost everything was done for two minutes."

And when the first plates of Andromeda were developed, what she found was that the stars on the outsides of the galaxy were not moving any slower than the stars near the center. This meant that

In the 1950s and '60s, when Vera first began working in astronomy, observatories were generally not open to women (although the national facilities were available to anyone whose proposal was accepted). At the Palomar observatory, the single bathroom on the ground floor said "Men." By 1990, annoyed that the sign was still there, Vera cut out a little paper figure with a skirt and taped it to the door.

the gravitational force was equally strong at the galaxy's outermost edges. Simply put, there must be substantial matter—of some sort—extending to the edge of the galaxy.

"The best explanation for what I was seeing was that the matter in the galaxy wasn't distributed as we had expected and assumed, but that there was lots of it far out—even though it wasn't bright," said Vera.

The very concept of matter that doesn't radiate, or shine, wasn't a concept at all. It simply hadn't been imagined. And hence another scientific controversy was born. But after Vera's study went on to include some sixty spiral galaxies, her observations and data were so clear, so precise, that by the 1980s astronomers and cosmologists had little choice but to embrace the newfound knowledge and begin to unravel its mysteries.

Vera Rubin's discovery of dark matter has completely changed the way we look at the universe. It is so much more vast and mysterious and intriguing than we had ever imagined. And our place within the universe is still undefined: how big is the universe? how did we get here? is there other life out there? Now, of course, the next task is to determine exactly what the dark matter is. Vera predicted that particle physicists would have an answer in ten years. That proved overly optimistic. It is, obviously, extremely difficult to study something that can't be seen. Whether dark matter consists of regular matter (known elements such as hydrogen and nitrogen) or of some new, exotic matter is still unknown. So the next time you happen to be peering out at the bright lights of the Milky Way—or even beyond—try looking at the stuff you can't see. That's where exciting new discoveries are just waiting to be made.

Observatories today are completely different from those in Vera's early days. The cold factor has been eliminated: astronomers now sit in a warm room on the floor of the telescope dome. There are no photographic plates to hand-develop because everything is done by computer. Two-minute songs, although no longer necessary, can still be sung.

Let's Start at the Very Beginning
Denise Schmandt-Besserat

Remember—as a little kid—learning to write your name? How at first your letters were shaky and squiggly? And remember counting . . . all the way from one to ten? Who taught you to write and to count? Who taught your teachers? Who taught those who taught them? How did it begin? Where did writing and counting come from?

Now, thanks to archeologist Denise Schmandt-Besserat, we know. Ten thousand years ago, in a time so distant it's referred to as prehistory, writing and counting developed—in tandem—in the region known as Mesopotamia (present-day Iraq). After nearly twenty years of research, Denise made a momentous discovery. She uncovered the very roots of writing, unmasked the very origins of counting. And, remarkably, her evidence showed—contrary to what was assumed—that counting actually preceded writing. Furthermore, the need to count was directly responsible for developing the ability to write. Denise discovered that writing emerged from an ancient counting device—little geometric-shaped clay tokens.

"We always knew we were missing what was happening before cuneiform," said Denise. *"Everybody was expecting something would come, but nobody was expecting that it would be three-dimensional. It was a big surprise!"*

What people were expecting was perhaps a simpler, more arcane cuneiform script.

But Denise did not originally set out to solve the mystery of early writing. As an archeologist, her main area of interest was the ancient Middle East. Particularly, she was interested in the materials that objects were made of. She was

Denise Schmandt-Besserat

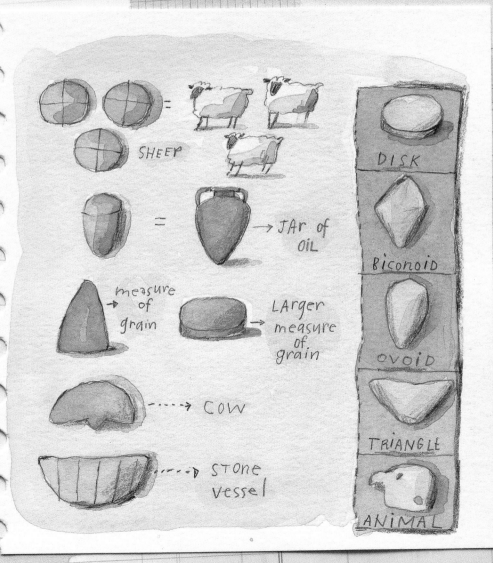

SHEEP

= → JAr of
OIL

measure
of
grain

LArger
measure
of
grain

----→ COW

----→ Stone
Vessel

DISK

BICONOID

OVOID

TRIANGLE

ANIMAL

enamored with the idea that she could see from millennium to millennium how materials were used, how they evolved, and how the technology grew. And even more specifically, she was intrigued by clay, primarily because of its ubiquitousness—it was literally found everywhere. Denise found clay objects in excavation collections from many countries, including Turkey, Syria, Lebanon, Jordan, Israel, Iraq, Iran, France, England, and Germany.

Cuneiform (kyoo-ne-form) was the first script, developed in the Middle East, to employ a specific, unique set of symbols unlike the images they represented. It utilized wedge-shaped strokes and was primarily written on clay tablets. The tokens Denise discovered were used to count goods 5,000 years before the invention of cuneiform.

In 1969, Denise decided to study ancient clay materials to establish when, how, and why the use of clay came about. So she traipsed from one Middle Eastern museum to the next, examining the clay collections from archeological site excavations.

"What I was looking for were the earliest possible bricks, pieces of hearth, figurines, and these kinds of things," Denise explained. *"And I did find lots of these things—some as old as 8000* B.C. *But each time, next to those figurines and pots, there was always a box that had these little clay objects that I had never heard of, that I was not expecting."*

Since these objects were made of clay and thus applicable to her study, she took note of them: measured them, sketched them, and identified the type of clay they were made from. She found spheres, cones, disks, tetrahedrons, and other shapes. She encountered these tokens in collections from every site in the Middle East, spanning an unbelievable 5,000 years. And no one knew what they were.

Denise's first breakthrough came from recognizing that the 10,000-year-old tokens were similar to much more complex counters found in cities that flourished 5,000 years later. Once she had an idea what her tokens were, Denise slowly began to put together the seemingly unrelated pieces of the puzzle. The archeological evidence suggested that with the birth of farming and agriculture (which replaced hunting and gathering) came the need for keeping track of goods.

As a young girl of nine, Denise showed the first inklings of archeological interest. In a souvenir shop her father said he would buy her one item; she chose an ancient, broken-up Roman lamp.

Each token shape, then, represented a specific good: a cone represented a small measure of grain, a sphere stood for a large measure of grain, and a disk was a sheep. The tokens were used in a one-to-one method of accounting—one token of a particular shape equaled one specific good (one disk = one sheep; two disks = two sheep, and so on).

Not only did prehistoric people create hundreds of new token shapes to count many kinds of goods, but they also came up with new ways to use them, such as keeping track of loans.

"If a person could not pay his debts, for example," said Denise, *"tokens were used to represent the amount that was due. And hollow clay balls, or envelopes, were later invented to store these IOUs."*

Clay envelopes, or *bullae*, were also used to secure transactions. When a deal was made, say, for the delivery of five bushels of grain at harvest time, the buyer and seller would have five tokens each— in this case, five spheres. And at harvest time, the buyer would match his five spheres one to one with the expected five bushels of grain. To ensure accuracy and prevent cheating, the tokens were sealed in a clay envelope to separate and secure them. So if a farmer accepted a delivery of five bushels of grain, he would break open the clay envelope and find five spheres: one sphere token for each bushel delivered. The tokens, then, were used to keep track of the amount and type of goods sold—as a receipt of sorts.

The tokens were an example of concrete counting— each token could count only one type of thing (a cone could only count small measures of grain, a sphere only large measures of grain). The Sumerians of Mesopotamia, in 5000 B.C., invented abstract counting by giving number values to the signs for grain: the impression of a cone stood for 1, a sphere represented 10, a large wedge indicated 60, and so on. For the first time, number and objects counted were separated, or abstracted.

"The fact that the first tokens coincided with the beginning of farming suggests that animal herding and agriculture made counting a necessity," Denise explained. *"It is not surprising that counting became important when people's survival over the winter months depended on the storage of goods and animal flocks, and knowing when the next crop necessitated putting aside seeds for sowing."*

Gradually, the farmers decided to make impressions of the tokens on the outside of the clay

The Evolution of Writing

8000–3000 B.C.		TOKENS USED for ACCOUNTING
3500–3200 B.C.		ENVELOPES
3200–3100 B.C.		IMPRESSED TABLETS
3100–2900 B.C.		PICTOGRAPHY OF TOKENS by STYLUS
3100–3000 B.C.		WRITING INVENTED in EGYPT (hieroglyphs)
2900 B.C.–300 A.D.		CUNEIFORM SCRIPT
1500 B.C.	PW⅄YN	invention of ALPHABET (in Phoenicia?) using only consonants
800 B.C.	ΣΔΟΚΗΑ	GREEK ALPHABET (with vowels)
600–500 B.C.	QVKE·PECV	Latin ALPHABET (Direct ancestor of ENGLISH ALPHABET)
500 A.D.	ﺍﻟﻌﺮﺑﻲ	Arabic inscriptions

envelope—again using a one-to-one correspondence—so that someone could tell exactly what was in the envelope without having to break it open. Eventually, it was realized that it was redundant to enclose the tokens in the marked envelope, so they simply made the impressions of the tokens on the outside. With nothing to put inside, the envelope itself became unnecessary and morphed into a flat tablet—and impressions of the tokens were made on it. With time, instead of making impressions, a pointed stylus, or stick, was used to trace the tokens on the tablet, which made them more distinguishable. And thus writing was born. Denise's research proved that the roots of writing could be traced to 8000 B.C.—5,000 years earlier than experts had previously thought!

"Early signs of writing were always thought to be pictographic—pictures of objects they represented," Denise explained. "Instead, they turned out to be pictures of tokens that represented goods."

Today, we write and count so automatically—integrating both into almost every aspect of our daily lives—that we forget writing and counting didn't always exist. With Denise Schmandt-Besserat's study of ancient clay tokens and her stunning discovery of the origins of writing and counting, thousands of years shrouded in mystery have been unveiled. No longer do we wonder whether writing appeared "out of thin air" or whether some person or group of people just sat down one day and decided to create it. Now, thanks to tokens invented 10,000 years ago, not only can you write your name, but you can also count the letters in it.

The Little Rover That Could
Donna Shirley

"Presently—and it was impossible to tell when the moment arrived—Mars ceased to be a planet floating in space, and became instead a landscape far below. . . . Then the ground was rushing up to meet him, there was a series of gentle bumps, and the machine rolled slowly to a standstill. He was on Mars."
—The Sands of Mars *by Arthur C. Clarke*

So the classic work of fiction goes. But alas, it is only that—fiction—since no person has yet set foot on another planet. The idea simply lingers in our imagination or clings to the page of a science fiction book. But we're getting closer—thanks to a cool little rover.

And it was definitely cool. Everyone said so. "Did ya see that little Mars rover? Cool, huh?" Although Sojourner was not exactly human—twenty-five pounds, six wheels, a solar panel, and a few other hi-tech bells and whistles—she *was* on Mars. Meandering around the planet's surface at the breakneck speed of a half-inch per second, the rover held millions of earthbound watchers captive as they followed her adventures with delight (and just a twinge of envy). None followed more closely than Donna Shirley, a program manager for NASA (National Aeronautics and Space Administration)

The name Sojourner was chosen through a "name the rover" contest open to kids all over the world. There were 3,500 entries, each accompanied by an essay on a heroine. The winner—Valerie Ambroise, age twelve—chose Sojourner Truth. Valerie concluded her winning essay, "Sojourner will travel around Mars, bringing back the truth."

Of the nine known planets in our solar system—Mercury, Venus, Earth, Mars, Jupiter, Saturn, Uranus, Neptune, and Pluto—scientists are most interested in exploring Mars, not only because of its alluring reddish tint and close proximity to Earth, but also in part because of the "Goldilocks Effect." About 4.5 billion years ago, Venus, Earth, and Mars were all similar, small, rocky planets. Yet somewhere along the way, Venus turned into a fiery inferno (too hot!) and Mars entered a permanent ice age (too cold!) while Earth settled into a moderate climate capable of supporting life (just right!). By understanding how Mars (and Venus) developed, scientists hope to better understand not only the formation of Earth and the secrets of its past, but also, hopefully, gain insights into its future.

and leader of the rover team. The very idea of using a small vehicle, a microrover, on a planetary mission was hers. And now her baby, Sojourner, was actually exploring the surface of Mars—trailblazing the way for future missions and perhaps creating the first real steppingstone toward human exploration.

"The most significant discovery of our mission was that small rovers can work on Mars," she said. "Nobody thought that they would—and Sojourner just worked fine."

When the words "Six wheels on soil!" registered, Donna's eyes welled with tears. She had dreamed—literally—of reaching the surface of Mars since she was a girl of twelve. Reading Arthur C. Clarke's *The Sands of Mars* freed her from her small Oklahoma town, took her high above the earth, and sent her soaring over the unexplored, windswept Martian landscape. Landing on Mars was a favorite scenario, replayed in her mind's eye again and again and again. By the 1990s, Donna was certain her dream could be a reality—and if she couldn't land herself, Sojourner would be the next best thing.

"People want to go to Mars for all different kinds of reasons," Donna said. "I always wanted to go to Mars because it was an unexplored, new place. Mars is really our next frontier. With the moon, you really can't live off the land. But Mars . . . maybe."

Donna's idea to send a microrover to Mars was originally dismissed as undoable. A rover needed to be big—like a Humvee truck—the argument went, so that it could traverse the surface without crashing into rocks or falling into craters or tipping over. It needed to be big to

Earth

mars

1997

Mars,
Milky Way

CURIOSITY

MICRO PLANETARY EXPLORATION

carry out sensitive scientific experiments. The bigger the rover, however, the bigger the bill. And "big" wasn't in the current NASA budget.

Donna was utterly convinced that the best chance for successful exploration lay with a small rover. A microrover would be considerably cheaper (Sojourner cost $25 million; other flight projects typically ran into the billions), faster to build (four years for Sojourner as compared with ten-plus years for other projects), and ultimately just as capable of carrying out experiments. Her greatest challenge was convincing others that it could be done—as well as finding the money to do it.

After many heated arguments, many trials, and many performances for top-level managers, the microrover was—at long last—given the green light to hitch a ride to Mars on the Pathfinder mission. Pathfinder was the space-flight vehicle that would land on the planet and, although unable to move, would conduct experiments of its own. Everything about Sojourner was micro: from her size (fully extended, she was just a foot tall) to the team Donna led (thirty people instead of the more typical three hundred to three thousand). But the time for small, in the world of space, had finally arrived. Small was good. Small was cheaper, faster, efficient . . . even fun.

"Designing the rover was like working a giant jigsaw puzzle," Donna wrote in her book Managing Martians, *"where six or eight boxes of puzzle pieces—representing all the solutions others had tried on previous missions to Mars—had been dumped on the table. We had to pick out those that would fit together and could be squeezed into our tiny margins of mass, power, and money."*

But squeeze they did, and on July 4, 1997, the Pathfinder spacecraft, carrying Sojourner, landed on the Martian surface. In all, the rover explored over 100 meters of Martian soil. And, despite getting stuck on rocks, having its main battery die, and experiencing communication problems, Sojourner was able to make a few remarkable discoveries of her own. The rover sent back 550 photographic images from the very surface of Mars and more than

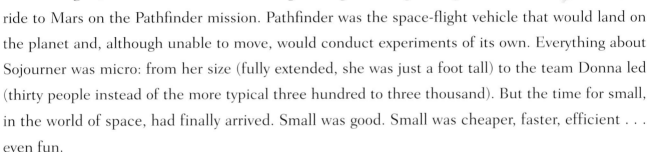

After the landing, enthusiasm for the rover reached a feverish pitch. Within a month, the mission's Web site logged 500 million hits. Mattel™ created a toy replica of the Sojourner rover, and demand was so strong the stores couldn't keep the toys in stock.

fifteen chemical analyses of rocks. She discovered rock conglomerates, which, upon further analysis, may very well support a theory that there was once an abundance of water on Mars.

After eighty-three days of spectacular exploration, Pathfinder and Sojourner lost communication with the ground crew. Since that day, they have remained on the frozen tundra of Mars, for they were never built for the expensive flight home.

But thanks in part to the little rover's exciting finds, scientists may be one step closer to determining whether water—and thus perhaps life—ever existed on Mars. And Donna Shirley's astounding discovery that microrovers can, in fact, successfully explore planetary surfaces has opened the door for many subsequent missions to Mars—rovers first, and then hopefully (as Donna predicts), down the line, humans.

"He had reached what to ancient man had been a moving red light among the stars, what . . . had been a mysterious and utterly unattainable world—and what was now the frontier of the human race."—The Sands of Mars

Perhaps in twenty (or thirty or forty) years our Martian explorer will burst out of the pages of science fiction and become a reality. Perhaps in twenty years that explorer will be you.

Tools in the Jungle
Jane Goodall

Cell phones, computers, skyscrapers, space stations. It's a hi-tech world out there with lots of hi-tech gadgets—each and every one of them constructed with tools. Throughout history, tools have literally made the world what it is today. No tools, no toys. No tools, no TVs . . . no houses, no cars. And, reaching farther back, without tools, humans would not have evolved. In the recent past, toolmaking was considered the distinctive characteristic that separated humans from the rest of the animal kingdom. No longer is that true.

They hoot. They grunt. They sleep in trees. But despite their differences, chimpanzees have some remarkable similarities to people. With a genetic makeup differing by about 1 percent from that of humans, they are our closest living relatives. In 1960, Jane Goodall traveled to Gombe Stream Game Reserve in Tanganyika (Tanzania, now), Africa, to observe chimpanzees in the wild—determined to learn everything she could about them. Within the first six months, Jane had made an astonishing discovery: chimpanzees in the wild used tools—grass stems to fish for termites, sticks to extend their reach or use as weapons. Later she saw them use leaves as sponges and napkins. Even more significantly, she discovered that chimps actually *made* tools! Jane's discoveries stunned the scientific community and not only forced us to reevaluate the very definition of a human being, but also gave us greater insight into, and understanding of, the only animal on our planet that shares 99 percent of our DNA.

"This discovery was followed by wider observations that chimpanzees in different

I have watched chimpanzees fish this way for two hours at a time, picking dainty morsels from the straw and munching them with delight.

1960

Tanganyika, Africa

CHIMPANZEES MAKE AND USE TOOLS

Jane Goodall

parts of Africa have different kinds of tool-using and tool-making behaviors," explained Jane. "And this led to realizing that chimps have a primitive kind of culture—that is, behaviors that are passed from one generation to the next, through observational learning."

The famed anthropologist Louis Leakey—in response to Jane's discovery that chimps were toolmakers—remarked, "Now we must redefine man, redefine tool, or accept chimpanzees as human."

When Jane arrived at Gombe, she knew next to nothing about chimpanzees—and even less about living among them in the wilderness. She had read the few existing books on behavior among captive chimps and from time to time had watched the two chimps at the London Zoo, but there was nothing extensive about her preparation. As a young girl, Jane had devoured animal books: she read *Tarzan* and *Dr. Dolittle* over and over again under the sheets with a flashlight when she was supposed to be asleep. So when she arrived at Gombe, what she brought was a lifelong love of animals and an overwhelming desire to learn about them firsthand.

When Jane first witnessed a chimpanzee using a tool, she was watching a male chimp she had named David Greybeard. Unfortunately, he had his back to her, and although she wasn't more than ten yards away she had to watch through thick tangles of jungle vegetation. All she could see was that he was picking up blades of grass and then pushing something and eating something. She found it hard to believe that what she thought she was seeing—David "fishing" for termites—was in fact actually happening.

"I went up afterward, when he'd gone, and there were these pieces of grass and twigs laid about and termites still moving about," Jane said. "So I tested it. I pushed one of the abandoned grass stems into the termite mound, and lo and behold, termites came out. And I could tell that, yes, he was using these as tools."

It wasn't long before Jane witnessed the actual toolmaking—the deliberate stripping of leaves and trimming of wide blades. During the termite season, Jane discovered that chimps will make and use tools several times a day. Sometimes, they'll carry a tool with them from one termite mound to the next. Jane's observations continually revealed that the chimps acted deliberately and purposefully.

"They will get the idea—'OK, termites'—look around, pick a piece of grass, and go off to a termite heap that's totally out of sight," Jane said.

She also observed the chimpanzees' ingenuity with leaves—using them as a sort of napkin to wipe blood or mud from themselves and as sponges to sop up water to drink. In order for the sponge to work, the chimp needed to chew the leaves, crumpling them, to make them more absorbent. Thus, another example of chimp toolmaking.

"And so," explained Jane, "in your different environments, you can imagine that these tool-using behaviors were stumbled upon by some chimps in the past, and because they were adaptive, the tools became a part of the group's repertoire."

But it wasn't just learned behaviors or established patterns that the chimps exhibited.

"We also see spontaneous responses to a problem in the wild," Jane explained.

Jane witnessed the chimpanzees' thought processes as she held a banana, offering it to an adult male named Mike. He was wary. First, he shook a fistful of straw angrily at her and one of the straws accidentally touched the banana. Immediately, he purposefully selected one of the straws to poke the banana, but it bent. So he picked a stick, which he then used to whack the banana from her hand. He got the idea for using a tool the moment he saw the straw touch the fruit.

Some scientists have hypothesized that, given enough time, chimpanzees might develop into makers of even more complex tools. Already, a chimp in captivity has learned five hundred signs of American Sign Language (ASL), thus demonstrating what the chimp brain is capable of achieving.

Over her forty years of study, Jane and her team have compiled the foundation of our current knowledge of chimpanzee behavior and capabilities. What

Chimpanzees are at home in various parts of tropical Africa. The average adult male chimpanzee weighs about 120 pounds and measures about four feet tall. Females are about the same height and average 90 to 100 pounds. A chimp's average life expectancy in the wild is between thirty-five and forty years. Chimpanzees express emotion—despair, fear, sadness, joy—and communicate nonverbally with one another using hugs, kisses, and pats on the back. Sixty years ago, chimpanzees in the wild numbered in the millions. Today, it is estimated that fewer than 200,000 remain—because of human interference.

began with a young animal-lover hoping to indulge her passion ended with remarkable discoveries that have forever changed what it means to be human. The uncertainties of her situation (the unpredictability of living in the wild; the worries about getting sufficient funds to continue her studies; the difficulties of getting close enough to the chimps to make observations) were all pushed aside. Her focus remained clear: learn about chimps. And with patience and persistence, she did.

"There's still so much to discover, all around us," said Jane. *"And even if something's been seen by someone, when you see it yourself for the first time, it is your own, new discovery. And you might see something differently."*

Today, we *use* tools to *make* tools. But while chimpanzee toolmaking is nowhere near as complex and sophisticated, it is a start—and it does make one wonder what else is possible.

dis-cov-er /dis-'kev-er/ vb dis-cov-ered;
dis-cov-er-ing

2. to be the first to find, learn of, or observe

Discovery may apply to something requiring exploration or investigation or to a chance encounter

1. to obtain knowledge of as through observation or study

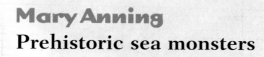

Mary Anning
Prehistoric sea monsters

As a young girl, Mary Anning walked the sea-swept beach of Lyme Regis, England, with her father, hunting for "curios" to sell to tourists. Curiosities, or curios, as some local townspeople called them, were more accurately known as fossils. The beach she searched was bordered by limestone and clay cliffs that were constantly eroding, or breaking apart—spilling their secrets down to the sand. In 1812, when Mary was about eleven years old, she made her first significant discovery: the fossil skeleton of an ichthyosaurus (meaning "fish-lizard")—an ancient dolphinlike reptile. In 1823, Mary made another astonishing discovery: the fossilized skeleton of a nine-foot-long "sea-monster" with a tiny five-inch head (like a turtle's), an unnaturally long neck, and four paddlelike feet. It was a near-complete plesiosaurus—between 65 and 215 million years old—that lived during the time of the dinosaurs. Mary's discovery—the first complete plesiosaurus ever found—was her greatest, and most significant, contribution to paleontology. Mary Anning continued to collect fossils in Lyme Regis (where tourists came as much to see her—now a famed fossil hunter), piling discovery upon discovery: *Pterodactylus macronyx* (flying lizard); another complete plesiosaurus; a squaloraja (a type of fossil fish); and many others. In a very real sense, hers was a lifetime full of discovery.

"As human beings we thrive on astonishment." ---Jean Fritz

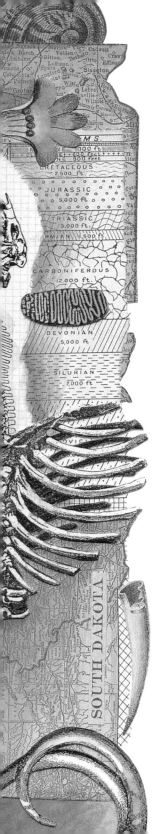

Biggest, Baddest, Best
Sue Hendrickson

The rescuers rushed to the cliff armed with scalpels and shovels. Stunned at what they saw—massive broken bones buried under rock—they dug in. In the sweltering hundred-plus-degree heat, they stabilized bones, swaddling each in a protective plaster cast.

Her teeth—sharp as razors—are longer than human hands. And she has sixty of them. She's as tall as the top of a basketball backboard and as long as one and a half school buses. She weighs more than a pile of elephants. And her age? Sixty-seven. That's sixty-seven *million* years old. Her name is Sue. She was discovered in August of 1990, near Faith, South Dakota, by explorer, adventurer, and fossil hunter extraordinaire Sue Hendrickson. "She" was the largest and most complete skeleton—with the best-preserved bones—of a *Tyrannosaurus rex* ever found.

The discovery of what would become the world's most famous dinosaur happened—as is often the case with discoveries—somewhat by chance. Were it not for a flat tire, and thus some spare time, Sue Hendrickson might never have ventured across seven miles of badlands toward an exposure of cliff that she felt had been "calling" her for two weeks. But she and her dog Gypsy took the three-hour hike, and within ten minutes of walking along the base of the cliff—head down, scanning the ground—she spotted bone fragments. It would be ten years

Dinosaur Sue is a nearly complete *T. rex*, with 90 percent of her skeleton recovered. The very first *Tyrannosaurus rex* to be discovered was unearthed in 1900, and since then about twenty *T. rex* specimens have been found. After Sue, the most complete *T. rex* is only 65 percent complete, and three others are about 45 percent complete. Of the remaining dinosaurs, we have just a handful of bones each.

before Sue the *T. rex* (named after her finder, of course) would be reassembled in all her glory, for all the world to see . . . to study, to learn from, to be *wowed* by.

"*I looked up to see where these bone fragments were coming from,*" *explained Sue.* "*Just above my head, about eight feet up, there were some bones sticking out of the hill. There were a number of bones there, but what was indicative of what it was were the three vertebrae in a line. These were very different bones than I was used to working with.*"

Sue knew they weren't *Triceratops*, nor were they duck-billed dinosaur bones, the kind she had been collecting in the preceding months. The bones were definitely dinosaur—evident not only by their enormous size but also by the fact that the geological stratum (layer of earth) in which the bones were embedded was known to be of the late Cretaceous period, when some dinosaurs still roamed the earth. She also knew that the bones belonged to a carnivorous, or meat-eating, dinosaur by the concave shape of the vertebrae (spinal bones) and the hollowness of the bone.

Many, if not most, things about the *T. rex* dinosaurs remain a mystery. Were they cold-blooded or warm-blooded? (They were previously thought to be cold-blooded, but recent studies are beginning to lean the other way.) Were they predators or scavengers? (Current studies suggest they were both.) What were their tiny forelimbs used for? (That's not known. Scientists do know, however, that these limbs were very powerful.) Are birds living dinosaurs? (It is a theory. Birds and dinosaurs share many similar skeletal features, and Sue's skeleton provided the first concrete evidence of a dinosaur wishbone, or furcula.) Is Sue a girl? (Currently the gender of a *T. rex* cannot be positively identified.)

"*I said to myself, 'OK, the only big carnivorous dinosaur alive at that time was* T. rex,*'*" *Sue recalled.* "*And I said, 'Wow! Here's part of a* T. rex.*' And then I said, 'But you don't* find T. rex—*you don't* see T. rex.*' I'm not normally a screamer, but I was* really *excited.*"

In a sense, it was the excitement of finding something incredible—not necessarily just a fascination with dinosaurs—that Sue Hendrickson had sought and had been seeking for a great many years. Born with what she calls "itchy feet," Sue has dreamed of faraway places, of faraway adventures, since she was a young girl. By the time she was a teenager, she decided to indulge her desire to roam and set off on a life of exploration. "A real Indiana Jones" is how a colleague once described

1990

Faith,
South Dakota

Sue Hendrickson

FOSSIL BONES OF T.REX

CURIOSITY

AGE : 67 million YEARS
LENGTH: 45 feet
HEIGHT: 13 feet
WEIGHT: 14,000 Pounds
NUMBER of TEETH : 60
NUMBER of BONES: 250
7½"-12"
T. Rex tooth

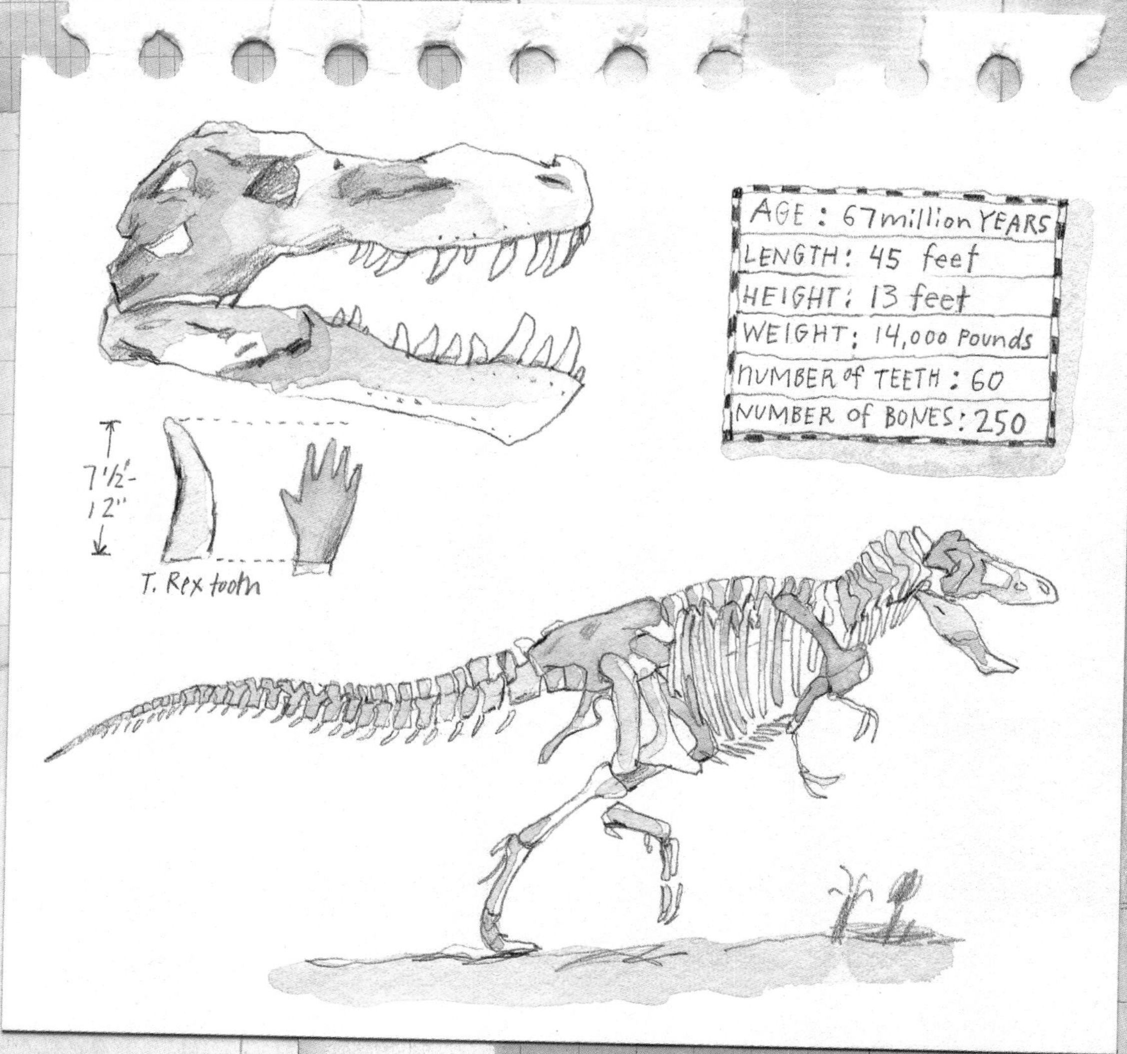

her. She has zipped around the world from one adventure to the next: underwater diving on the expedition that discovered the lost city of Alexandria, Egypt; exploring sunken battleships from the 1700s; searching for amber (and the prehistoric insects often trapped inside) in the mountains of the Dominican Republic; and, of course, hunting dinosaur fossils.

"I've been the luckiest person I know," Sue said. *"Not just lucky in finding things, but in being able to work on really great projects with the freedom to just up and go to whatever interests me."*

Whether it's a sixth sense or unbelievable luck, Sue doesn't know. But she does know she's always been just darn good at finding things. So when she happened upon the *T. rex* in the hillside, it didn't seem completely outside the realm of possibility.

She went to get her colleague Pete Larson, head of the Black Hills Institute (a commercial fossil-hunting firm that she was working with), and brought him to the site first. He *was* a screamer. Sue said he jumped up and down, yelling "It's all there! I just know it's all there!" It took Sue, Pete, and four other people seventeen days to excavate, or remove, the entire dinosaur. Before removing any fossils, though, the crew documented everything with still photographs, video, and hand-drawn maps.

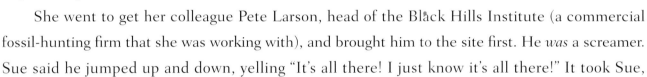

The Field Museum of Chicago, with assistance from the McDonald's® Corporation and Walt Disney World Resort®, purchased Sue the *T. rex* for $8.36 million. Sue is on permanent display at The Field Museum. Three identical life-size casts—replications of the bones—have been created: one will be on display in DinoLand U.S.A. at Walt Disney World Resort, and two will be part of a traveling exhibition for the McDonald's Corporation's millennium celebration, appearing at science museums and centers throughout the nation.

"Then we went up the side of the cliff to stabilize the bones sticking out so they wouldn't break any more," Sue said. *"After they're stabilized, you cover them and put on a plaster jacket—just like a plaster cast on your leg—so it's got a hard surface to help get it safely back to a prep lab."*

After the excavation, Sue said goodbye to the greatest discovery of her life. She gave it to Pete as a going-away present and moved on to new projects of adventure and discovery. (Leaving her dinosaur was the hardest thing she ever did, but her "itchy feet" like to keep moving.) Seven years after Sue the *T. rex* was discovered, she was put up for auction—for sale to the highest bidder, with all the proceeds going to the owner of the land where she was found.

Scientists now have an unprecedented opportunity to learn more about the biggest, baddest, not to mention best, *T. rex* ever found—to learn more about how it grew and moved and ate; how it used its senses; what its relationship was with other dinosaurs . . . and countless other mysteries. After 67 million years, thanks to the keen eyes of Ms. Hendrickson, Sue is once again up on her humongous legs ready to greet the world. Anyone speak dinosaur?

The Longest Day of the Year
Anna Sofaer

Ahh . . . summer. Sunshine and lemonade. Bike rides and boat rides; ball games and outdoor concerts. For most of us, summer begins with the first whiff of warm air or the last bong of a school bell. But there is an actual first day of summer. It says so right on the kitchen calendar.

A thousand years ago, with no glossy paper calendar to consult—for that matter, with no paper and no known written language—the Anasazi Indians of Chaco Canyon, New Mexico, knew precisely when the first day of summer, the summer solstice, had arrived. They marked it with a dagger of light on a wall of rock. For a dozen or so generations, their hand-made calendar—which marked the summer and winter solstices and the spring and autumn equinoxes—went unnoticed. And then, in 1977, artist Anna Sofaer happened by. What caught her eye was a piercing dagger of light—so striking and vivid—cutting through the center of a spiral petroglyph carved on the canyon rock face.

"I was so interested in rock art," Anna said, *"and I had seen in a little newsletter that volunteers were wanted for the archival recording of rock art in Chaco Canyon."*

Anna had worked for years as an artist—sculpting and painting—before she became captivated by photography, with its intoxicating ability to capture and manipulate shadow and light. Her artistic play with light and shadow, along with an interest in prehistoric cultures, led her to take an archeo-astronomy class (a new branch of science combining archeology and

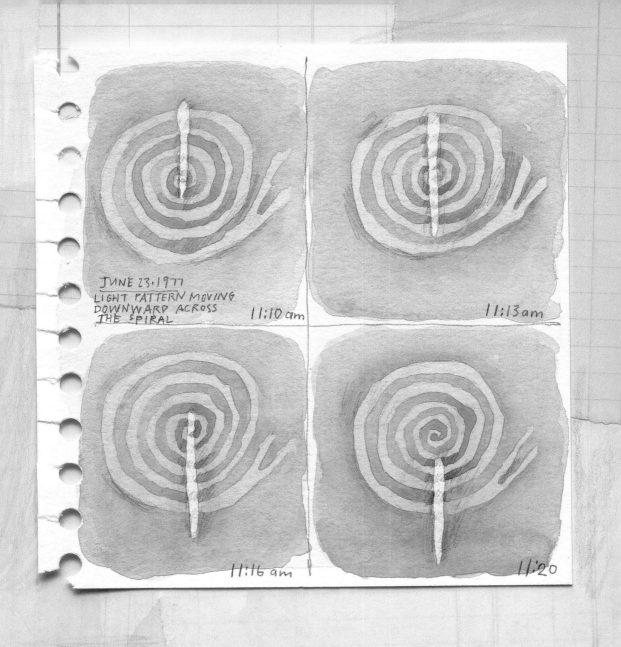

JUNE 23·1977
LIGHT PATTERN MOVING
DOWNWARD ACROSS
THE SPIRAL

11:10am

11:13am

11:16am

11:20

1977   Chaco Canyon,
New Mexico

SUN DAGGER CALENDAR

astronomy), which in turn introduced her to rock art in the Southwest.

And so it happened that in late June, Anna joined a workshop that was camping out in beautiful Chaco Canyon, searching for art on canyon walls. On the second day of the excursion, Anna volunteered with a partner to climb the highest elevation in the canyon, Fajada Butte, which rises 135 meters above the valley floor. With the temperature reaching over 100 degrees and the ever-present rattlesnakes lurking in the canyon crevices, they climbed and photographed all the rock art they encountered. Anna passed by the calendar, noticed the spiral art carved on the rock—which was in shadow—and decided to come back when there was more light to photograph it properly.

"The next day, we happened to get there near noon," explained Anna. "And there was this magnificent dagger of light right through the center [of the spiral petroglyph]. It was such a strong image—being bisected at that moment—that you just couldn't think it was casual or accidental."

Summer solstice marks the longest day of the year, the time when the sun is at its highest point in the sky. It falls on or near June 21. Winter solstice, marking the shortest day of the year, the time when the sun is at its lowest point in the sky, is around December 21. The spring and autumn equinoxes—around March 21 and September 23, respectively—mark the times when the sun crosses the equator and day and night are of equal length everywhere. Other ancient solstice markers have been found—most famously, Stonehenge in Great Britain—but no other markers like the sun-dagger calendar have been found, marking the sun at its highest point both in the day (at noon) and in the year.

Had she arrived just three minutes later, the dagger of light would not have been so brilliant; the image, not so dramatic. But by chance she was there at precisely the right time, on precisely the right day, in precisely the right time of the year. And she photographed it. *"I remember saying to my partner, 'It's marking the highest point of the sun in the day and the year. It must be a solstice marker.'"*

Discovering the dagger-bisected spiral—and the smaller spiral off to the side—was step one. Step two was to determine—and prove—that it really was a solstice marker by uncovering how it worked and how, in all likelihood, it had come to be.

"It was easy in a certain way," said Anna. "It was a matter of being there every month and carefully record-

ing what happened—what light patterns occurred there. When we went back at the equinox, there was a marking; at the winter solstice, there was a marking."

Through her detailed recordings Anna was ultimately able to prove that the sun calendar was indeed solstitial (in fact, it turned out to be a sophisticated lunar marker as well). But Anna created a great brouhaha in the scientific community when she suggested that the three giant stone slabs that filtered the light to form the dagger had been deliberately moved into position by the Anasazi. Experts argued that such a scheme was far too elaborate and that the stones were far too large to have been moved by the simple Pueblo people.

Why the Anasazi needed to mark time with such precision remains unknown. The calendar was presumably used for a multitude of purposes: to time the planting of seasonal crops, to mark the arrival of ceremonial observances, and to generally measure the passage of time. It is known, through oral tradition, that the sun played a central and crucial role in the lives of the Anasazi people. It was revered as a source not only of light but of life. The Anasazi measured the meaning of their existence—of their place in the cosmos—with regard and respect to the sun.

Ultimately, a geologist determined that the three stone slabs had at one time been attached to each other as a block unit and that the block had been attached—horizontally—to the face of the cliff several feet to the left of where the individual vertical slabs now stood. This was proof that the slabs had indeed been moved and thus was a clear indicator that the Anasazi people were capable of the complex calculations and precise planning necessary to create such an intricate calendar.

With the unmasking of this sun-dagger calendar, Anna opened a window to the lives of these ancient Native American people (ancestors of the present-day Pueblo Indians)—supplying evidence of their extraordinary efforts to create and maintain a harmonious life through the interconnectedness of art, science, and religion. She has brought the lives of the Anasazi into sharper focus. They had no math (as we understand it today), yet were able to make precise, advanced mathematical calculations; they had no engineering, yet were able to understand and manipulate the properties of matter and energy; they had no writing, yet their art and craftsmanship continue to communicate chapters of their story. It is a story of sophistication, masked by simplicity. A story of people who, not unlike ourselves, welcomed the first day of summer.

My, What Big Teeth You Have
Mary Leakey

The family tree: it is a tangled treasure trove of great-great-grandmothers who were pioneers and third-cousins-once-removed who fought in the Civil War and great-grandfathers who immigrated by boat. In an effort to learn about those who came before and to learn how we ourselves arrived in the present, many of us undertake the study of our personal histories, tracing our ancestors back through time.

Where *did* we come from? It is *the* ultimate question. But to find out, to really find out—to get back to the beginning—we need to trace our roots not just back through decades and centuries, but back through the millennia, back hundreds of thousands of years—and then back further, and further still . . . .

For nearly thirty years, archeologist Mary Leakey searched on hands and knees through the stone and silt of Olduvai Gorge in northern Tanganyika (now Tanzania) in East Africa, looking for fossil remains of early humans, or hominids, as they are called. Hominids are prehumans directly on the human ancestral tree.

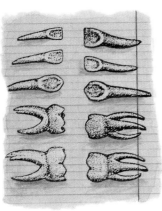

On a blistering hot day in July of 1959, she found one—a hominid skull. She saw the gigantic teeth first, poking out from beneath the dirt. It was a breathtaking find, and it turned out to be 1.75 million years old! That discovery alone extended the date of human origins twofold.

"It came about that on the morning of 17 July I went out by myself, with the two Dalmatians Sally and Victoria, to see what I could find of interest . . . ," wrote Mary in her

OLDUVAI GORGE

The teeth were projecting from the rock

AFRICA

TANGANYIKA

ZINJ --- Zinjanthropus boisei
1.75 million years old

Because of the powerful jaw and skull, Zinj was nicknamed, "Nutcracker Man."

1959 | Tanganyika, Africa

HOMINID SKULL

CURIOSITY

MARY LEAKEY

In 1859, a century before her discovery, the renowned biologist Charles Darwin published his landmark book *On the Origin of Species,* which presented the theory of evolution by natural selection. It was greeted by a cacophony of criticism. The theory of evolution holds that plants and animals (including humans) have developed from other kinds of earlier plants and animals and that the differences between the species of today and yesterday are the result of inherited changes occurring over the course of thousands of years.

autobiography, Disclosing the Past. *"I turned my steps towards a site not far west of the junction of the two gorges, where we knew that bones and stone artefacts were fairly common on the surface . . ."*

The Dalmatians were her constant companions, not only at Olduvai Gorge, but throughout her life from the time she was a teenage girl. (So central were the Dalmatians in Mary's life that she dedicated her autobiography "To the Dalmatians, past and present, who have so greatly enriched my life with their companionship, intelligence and loyalty.") It was around age sixteen that Mary began attending archeology lectures—informally and independently—in an attempt to train herself in her newly chosen career. She was first introduced to the world of prehistory when she was about ten. With her parents, she toured the archeology collections of various European museums, and before long she and her father were invited by a friend from a French museum to visit an actual archeological excavation. There, she was allowed to sift through heaps of dug-out dirt, searching for treasures. The thrill of discovering ancient artifacts—the thrill of the treasure hunt itself—was wonderfully seductive. She didn't know at the time that she would eventually pursue archeology, but she did know what she liked.

Typically, Mary worked alongside her husband, anthropologist and archeologist Louis Leakey. But on this particular day in July of 1959, he was ill and had remained in camp, in bed. She had promised some nearby filmmakers that they could film one of the excavations from start to finish, so the site she had originally planned to excavate was put on hold until the cameraman arrived. So this morning, Mary was examining a different site—site FLK. In a way, just killing time.

"One scrap of bone that caught and held my eye was not lying loose on the surface but projecting from beneath," Mary wrote. *"It seemed to be part of a skull, including a mastoid*

process (the bony projection below the ear). It had a hominid look, but the bones seemed enormously thick—too thick, surely. I carefully brushed away a little of the deposit, and then I could see parts of two large teeth in place in the upper jaw. They were hominid. It was a hominid skull . . . and there was a lot of it there."

Mary raced back to camp, announcing her arrival with exuberant outbursts of *"I've got him! I've got him!"* The next nineteen days were spent removing tons of rock and sifting through all of it to be certain they weren't missing anything. For hours on end Mary and Louis worked on their knees with delicate tools—including a small camelhair brush and a dental pick—gently prying the skull Louis christened *Zinjanthropus boisei*—or Zinj, for short—from his resting place of nearly two million years. In archeology, one seldom finds fossil skulls whole, and Zinj was no exception. Zinj came in nearly four hundred fragments, including two of the largest molars that had ever been seen, and Mary had the excruciatingly difficult task of putting him back together bit by bit. But when she finished, she had a complete skull, minus only the lower jaw. And when specialists applied a new—and extremely accurate—dating technique to rock samples found near Zinj (known as potassium-argon dating), they discovered his astonishing age.

Mary Leakey's discovery and subsequent study of Zinj revealed a wealth of information: the 1.75-million-year-old hominid was bipedal (walked upright), lived exclusively on the ground, used and possibly made tools, possibly had a home base of sorts, and probably shared food with fellow hominids. It turned out, however, that he didn't belong on the main branch of the human tree but rather on a side branch of australopithecines (southern ape human)—specifically *Australopithecus robustus*—

Seventeen years after the discovery of Zinj, elsewhere in Tanzania—Laetoli, to be exact—Mary's efforts (along with her team's) yielded one of the most spectacular discoveries in all of paleoanthropology: two parallel trails of hominid footprints. It was an extraordinary piece of evidence: unquestionable proof that our hominid ancestors were fully bipedal (walked upright) 3.5 million years ago. And these ancient ancestors left behind a very modern looking footprint: a fully shaped heel, a strong arch, and a straight big toe (not out to the side like an ape's). A great, straight, humanlike big toe.

human evolution

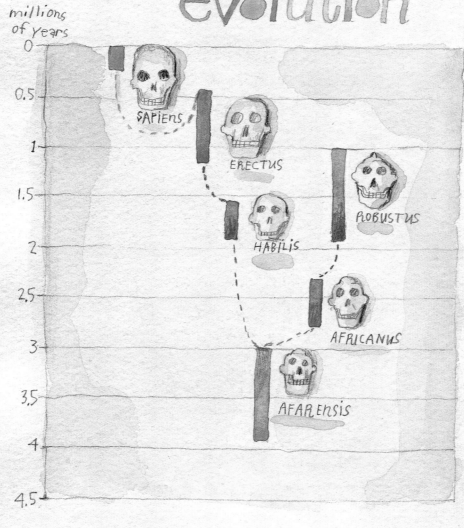

millions
of years

0

0.5

1

1.5

2

2.5

3

3.5

4

4.5

SAPIENS

ERECTUS

HABILIS

ROBUSTUS

AFRICANUS

AFARENSIS

A hominid is loosely defined as a human ancestor: either an extinct ancestor, a relative, or a true human. It is safe to say that hominids were erect-walking primates, and many were toolmakers. *Homo sapiens* are true humans (the word *sapien* means 'thinking man'). A *Homo sapien* might be defined as possessing self-awareness: being smart enough to recognize oneself as human. All human beings are hominids, although not all hominids are human.

that eventually became extinct. Humans and Zinj did share a common ancestor, *Australopithecus afarensis*, but it is from Zinj's contemporary, *Homo habilis*, that humans are believed to have eventually evolved. Free at last from thousands of tons of rock, Zinj's gigantic teeth promptly chomped a bite out of the human ancestral tree—leaving teethmarks that were the turning point in the study of human origins.

On the Road Again
June Moxon

A train and an unidentified thingamajig leave the station at the same time. They both travel 4,000 miles. If the train travels at 50 miles per hour and arrives at the destination in 80 hours, how long does it take the thingamajig to get there traveling a mere 3 miles per hour?

Answer: a whopping 1,333 hours (not including stops!)

Of course there were faster ways to go. Not to mention easier ways. But artist June Moxon couldn't think of a more interesting way to travel across the United States coast to coast. So in the summer of 1989, June, with her friend Ken and their dog, Scratchin'-Itchin'-Lickin'-Bitin'-Snortin'-Black-and-White-Cow Dog (or Scratch, for short), set out from Ferndale, California, in a four-piece, thirty-seven-foot-long, two-thousand-plus-pound, outrageous contraption known as a kinetic sculpture. And they began to pedal. And they would continue to pedal at least six hours a day until they reached their destination on the other side of the country. Along the way, June would discover something completely unexpected—the genuine kindness of strangers. And by the time she was through, more than two years later, she had discovered a novel—albeit tiring—way to traverse the United States.

It all began with a free ticket to Hobart Brown's annual Kinetic Sculpture Race in Ferndale. June arrived, ticket in hand, to take her newly awarded place on Brown's kinetic sculpture. She went to the race out of simple curiosity. What she found was dozens of hard-working, hard-playing individuals racing homemade, wildly artistic contraptions across thirty-eight miles of the most problematic race course imaginable.

"It's very difficult," June explained. *"It's twelve miles of sand dunes. There are three miles of water and a great big huge mud bog. It's very intense. It takes about seven hours just to get through the first day."*

"Kinetic" refers to motion, and kinetic art is defined as art (usually, but not exclusively, sculptural) that includes mechanical parts that can be set in motion. The power to propel that motion may come from a motor or from wind or, as with June's kinetic sculpture, the motion may be people-powered.

Within the first block of her first race, the sculpture June was on—the People-Powered Bus—broke down, and the crew, including June, ended up pushing and pulling their weighty contest entry the entire distance. They raced not for money, ribbons, or trophies but "for the glory." The contest was a great display of creativity and engineering prowess as well as a fabulous display of lightheartedness. June was hooked.

"After that first day, I knew there was no way I'd ever stop doing this," said June. *"It just gets in your bones—so many people having so much fun."*

She has been building and racing kinetic sculptures ever since. And at first, she was the only woman racer who built her own machines. By 1989, she was ready for a new adventure.

"No one had ever gone across the United States in a kinetic sculpture before," said June. *"We felt that sooner or later someone would, and we wanted to make sure that whoever did it did it on an artistic machine—so we just decided it might as well be us."*

It took three years of planning and building before they were able to hit the road. The finished sculpture was a sight to be seen: Ken's "castle" and June's "shoe" (a snakeskin-covered high heel) built over reconfigured tricycles, pulling a round barrel (the sleeping quarters) and, at the back, a suitcase carrier (for miscellaneous junk). June and Ken called the contraption, simply, Kinetic Sculptures Across America.

For June, coming up with the design for her sculpture was a no-brainer. The fact is, June is obsessed with shoes. She boasts more than five hundred

Kinetic
SCULPTURE | 2000 lbs.
37 feet long

CALIFORNIA FLORIDA

1989-
1991

Ferndale, California-
St. Augustine, Florida

CROSSING AMERICA IN A KINETIC SCULPTURE

CURIOSITY

June Moxon

pairs of footwear, and that includes only the wearable versions. Instead of wallpaper, at least one room in her house is covered from top to bottom with hanging shoes: chunky ones, clunky ones, rhinestone-covered ones . . . you name it. So when June set out to create a kinetic sculpture that would carry her across the country, she wanted something that was not only artistically attractive but also representative of her personality.

"We left town with two hundred dollars," June said. *"We knew we were going to have to work our way across the U.S. A lot of the time, we'd do trades. Like with the A & W, we'd paint Christmas scenes all over their windows and then we'd get free food."*

June undertook the journey to satisfy her curiosity. The novelty and adventure of doing something that had never before been done—of finding out something she had never before known: how to cross the United States on a kinetic sculpture—was compelling and alluring. And her journey did not disappoint. Everywhere June and Ken went—Oregon, Idaho, Wyoming, Utah, Colorado, Kansas, Oklahoma, Texas, Louisiana, Mississippi, Alabama, Florida—they were met with incredulous stares and dazed expressions. Kinetic Sculptures Across America often caused traffic jams as people stopped their cars to have a look. *"If there were any people around,"* said June, *"they were usually somewhere around us."* Everywhere they went, people bought them lunch or breakfast or dinner or snacks and drinks. Everywhere they went, people offered the use of their bathrooms—and, thankfully, their showers.

"We would wake up in the morning and outside the barrel there would be a little note saying, 'Come down to the second house on the right—bring your laundry,'" explained June.

What would an adventure be without problems? June and Ken certainly had their share. Chains fell off, tires went flat . . . and Ken broke his leg. The broken leg threatened to end their trek—after all, it took two to propel that two-thousand-pound sculpture. But with

The base of June's high-heeled shoe was constructed from adult-sized, custom-made tricycles and a mishmash of other bicycle gear. The artistic portions were made of chicken wire and papier-mâché. The four-piece kinetic sculpture had thirty-two wheels and thirty-six gears. It could be pedaled on land or in water, and it had a solar panel that provided sporadic power to a CB, a radio, a teeny TV, and a fan for Scratch.

a bit of ingenious improvisation, they rigged their arms and legs together so that the force on the pedal would come from both the arm and the leg.

June's cross-country adventure landed her on CNN three times, on local news programs more than twenty times, in six magazines, including *National Geographic World,* and in over one hundred newspapers along the route.

For June, discovering how to cross the States on a sculpture was a process that revealed itself bit by bit, mile by mile. Each day was different—a discovery in its own right. The demands and limitations of the kinetic sculpture were impossible to predict. And the environment they pedaled through was equally unpredictable: snowstorms, rain, sleet, monstrously steep hills, frighteningly narrow bridges, and scores of unknown people and personalities.

"I see myself as both an explorer and an adventurer," June said, *"and, under protest, an athlete. Finishing it was a relief. There was such pleasure in accomplishing something."*

By the end of the journey, she was both exhausted and exhilarated. June Moxon had found an unprecedented way to get across America, and her kinetic-sculpture excursion had offered her a rare glimpse into the lives of countless people along the route. She experienced things up close and personal that she wouldn't even have seen had she traveled by train, plane, or automobile: fire ants in Texas, bear wrestling in Louisiana, and "tornado alley" in Oklahoma (in a paper vehicle!). On the highway, a Pepsi semitrailer truck pulled over and gave her free Pepsi for the road. She even saw her name in lights—on a sign at the dog races in Georgia: "Welcome June, Ken, and Scratch. Good Luck on your journey across America." And she did have good luck—luck, and a thingamajig.

Chapter Three

cu-ri-os-i-ty /kyur-e-as-te/ n,pl-ties

a desire to know or learn

"If we would have new knowledge we must get a whole world of new questions"
-- Susanne K. Langer

Maria de Sautuola
Paleolithic cave art

"Toros pintados!" exclaimed the child. In 1879, in a recently discovered cave on her family's estate in Altamira, Spain, young Maria de Sautuola wandered out of the dimly lit main chamber where her father was busy digging for ancient stone artifacts. While she was exploring, she found a small crawlspace that led to a hidden alcove. She scooted through. *"Toros pintados!"* she yelled. ("Painted bulls!") Her father followed her voice to the small room where she stood holding a candle and pointing in amazement at the paintings on the ceiling. It was an astonishing discovery. The painted animals were actually extinct bison, not bulls, and were unlike any cave art ever before found. Later, it was determined that the cave paintings of Altamira were 15,000 years old—from the Stone Age. Maria's discovery cast a new light on the ancient Stone Age people and was a remarkable milestone in art history.

Rachel Friedstein, Jessica Berenblum, Lauren Schulz, Raina Tripp
Heavy backpacks cause back injury

Backpacks are a way of life. Kids stuff their books, notebooks, folders, and miscellaneous junk into a pack, sling it ever so coolly over one shoulder, and off they go. But in 1998, four eighth-grade girls discovered the potential lifelong damage that backpacks can cause. They learned that 25 to 33 percent of adolescents experience lower back pain. And they found that heavy backpacks—and the improper use of them—will cause more severe back problems as adults. The girls learned that a fully packed backpack should weigh less than 10 percent of a person's body weight (less than eight pounds for an eighty-pound kid) and that both straps absolutely must be worn to avoid painful back trouble. The girls suggest that frequent locker stops can help lighten the load. The team has embarked on a Light Is Right awareness campaign to educate fellow students on their findings.

The power to question is the basis of all human progress

---Indira Gandhi

a desire to know or learn

Get the Lead Out
Katie Murray

The city's houses are old, the apartments worn. It's no surprise to see the outside paint cracking and crumbling—sloughing off paint chips that then mix in with the surrounding soil. It might be a surprise, though, to learn that most houses painted before 1977 were coated not only with the latest shades of blue, brown, or brick red, but also with primarily lead-based paint—which was poisonous.

Intrigued by a talk about lead poisoning given at an Earth Day celebration at her local zoo (she would later write in her logbook: *Saw exhibit on lead. Very Dangerous! Decided to do science project . . .*), Katie Murray took it upon herself to search out more information and explore the hazards of lead poisoning. Katie was just eleven years old when, in 1998, she decided to formulate and test an original hypothesis about lead poisoning in vegetables. Through her efforts, Katie discovered that potentially harmful levels of lead could find their way into home-grown vegetables—vegetables that people would probably eat.

"My dad works with a man who plants vegetables in the inner city, in community gardens," Katie said as she explained how she came up with her idea. *"Ms. Maher, a health department nurse at the zoo, had talked about inner cities—how bad lead poisoning is there—and so I wanted to see if those plants that were planted in the lead-contaminated soil, if when you ate them, you would be poisoned."*

Katie's love of science had really taken hold the previous year. When she was a fifth-grader, she did a science project, "Paper or Plastic?" about which type of grocery bag was better from an environmental standpoint. She won several awards. (As with her lead project, Katie did her fifth-grade project and entered it in science

Katie Murray

fairs on her own because her school didn't offer science-fair opportunities.) Now, armed with a small spiral notebook to log her progress, Katie began to find out about lead poisoning. Getting the lead—which is unavailable to the general public—proved to be a challenge. But after several phone calls, she was finally able to obtain it with the help of her sixth-grade science teacher. She first planted six different vegetables in both lead-contaminated soil and regular potting soil. But in the lead-contaminated soil, only two plants—the tomatoes and green peppers—survived.

"I called around to see if anyone could test them for me, because I didn't have the equipment. Finally I called the FDA and a man there named Mr. Hughes said that he would test them," explained Katie. "So I brought the plants to him and he cut them up—it was a long process he had to go through—and then he used a spectrograph test, and that's how he found out how much lead was in them."

Mr. Hughes, a chemist at the Food and Drug Administration (FDA), was stunned. His tests showed that Katie's green peppers had a lead content of .131 parts per million, while the tomatoes contained .06 parts of lead per million. The established safety standard for children is .08; anything above that is considered dangerous.

"Although the tomato was under the limit," Katie said, "it was under by such a small amount that Mr. Hughes said if children were to eat it, they would probably get lead poisoning. So it's still an unsafe amount."

What shocked the experts was that Katie's vegetables survived at all. It had always been assumed that plants containing high levels of lead would simply die before producing tempting, edible vegetables.

Katie Murray's discovery of potentially harmful lead levels in home-grown vegetables earned her nine

According to the Centers for Disease Control and Prevention, the number-one environmental health problem for children in the United States is lead poisoning. Young children (babies to preschoolers) are the ones most affected. Exposure to low levels of lead may cause learning disabilities, hearing loss, delayed growth, and a lower IQ. Exposure to higher lead levels may cause anemia, kidney problems, convulsions, coma, and even death.

awards, including a First Place Plaque at the Greater Kansas City Science and Engineering Fair and selection as a finalist for the "Discovery Young Scientist Challenge." Her discovery also prompted a prominent toxicologist to encourage Katie to publish her work in scientific journals, and he is helping her to do just that.

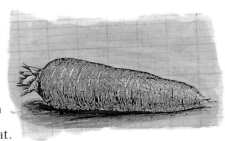

Up in Smoke
Klara, Eli, Erin, Lindsey

To everything there is a season (especially for allergy and asthma sufferers): the ragweed season (ah-choo!); the pollen season (wheeze, gasp); and in the Pacific Northwest, there's also the bluegrass burning season (ah-choo! scratch scratch, wheeze, cough . . . gasp . . . gasp).

In an effort to eliminate pests and disease, farmers in the Pacific Northwest annually burn their bluegrass fields. This can be problematic. The burning process releases harmful smoke particles into the community, causing complications for people who suffer from allergies, asthma, or cystic fibrosis. So Klara Bowman, Eli Penberthy, Erin Richardson, and Lindsey Watts—eighth-graders at Sacajawea Middle School in Spokane, Washington—decided to adopt this problem for their science-fair project. And in 1997, they discovered an alternative method for getting rid of unwanted bluegrass—by turning it into paper.

"At that time, in the newspaper, there were a lot of articles and controversies around grass burning," explained Lindsey. *"So we all decided maybe we could find a positive solution that would be a win-win for everyone."*

Through their research efforts, the girls learned of a Canadian man who had a successful business turning rice straw into paper.

"Rice and wheat and the bluegrass that we worked with all have a similar fiber," said Eli. *"So we thought, if he was doing it with rice straw, why couldn't we do it with bluegrass straw?"*

They contacted the Canadian man, who was very helpful. He told them about his paper-making process and helped them determine what chemicals they would need. The girls spent the next two months working in their classroom under the

cut the straw from the bluegrass

BALE THE STRAW 1.

Mix BLUEGRASS STRAW WITH CHEMICALS. COOK.

CHEMICALS 2.

BLUE GRASS
[Poa compressa]

BLEACH this PULP 3.

DIP SCREEN INTO PULP
LET EXCESS PULP DRIP OFF

4.
iron the screen
cloth-covered
PAPER

1997

Spokane, Washington

CURIOSITY

MAKE PAPER FROM BLUEGRASS STRAW

guidance of their teacher. They mixed bluegrass straw with various chemicals and cooked it to create pulp; experimented with the different pulps created; bleached the pulp; and ultimately turned the pulp into paper.

"The paper we made can be used for anything—in computers or whatever," Klara explained. *"You can't tell any difference between our paper and paper made from trees."*

Although their process for making paper would cost slightly more than traditional methods, the girls felt confident that because it was so environmentally safe, people would be willing to pay a bit more for their paper to help out their community. As an added benefit, their method actually helps the environment indirectly because, unlike traditional paper-making, it doesn't require the cutting of trees. After their experimentation, the girls wrote up their research and conclusions in a report, prepared a five-minute presentation, and designed a booth to demonstrate their project for the Bayer/NSF (National Science Foundation) science competition. In May 1997, Klara, Eli, Erin, and Lindsey won the top prize, the Bayer/NSF Award for Community Innovation, which provided $25,000 to implement their idea. Building a pulping mill in Spokane would cost millions of dollars—obviously not within the girls' means—so they did the next best thing.

"They gave us the money," Eli said, *"and we decided to use it to start a public awareness campaign. We made a video and we did a lot of presentations around the community. We really tried to get the word out about the grass-burning problem and our proposed solution to it."*

And the word did get out. Their discovery of a viable alternative to bluegrass burning not only garnered praise from community leaders and local political leaders but also caught the attention of a Hollywood screenwriter. He bought the rights to their story and is currently negotiating with a major studio to produce a movie loosely based on their experiences—to be titled something like *Science Girls.*

"In a way, it's kind of ironic," Erin said. *"None of us ever originally thought of ourselves as science-minded people."*

It seems that discovery—once again—is filled with unexpected surprises.

Drinkable Puddles
Rachael Charles

For most Americans, getting water is as easy as turning on the tap or pushing a button on the fridge. So reliable is our access to fresh water that we forget—or perhaps have never been aware—that clean, safe drinking water simply is not available to everyone. An eighth-grader thinks that should change.

While researching a project for science class, fourteen-year-old Rachael Charles was drawn to the pressing problem of undrinkable water in many parts of the world. What she found was shocking: an estimated *one billion* people throughout the world have unsafe drinking and bathing water. The water is chock full of harmful bacteria, such as *E. coli* and similar organisms, that can cause devastating diseases, primarily of the diarrheal variety. Rachael learned that unsafe water claims the lives of nearly 4 million children every single year. In addition, it causes nearly 900 million people to become severely ill each year. Boiling water kills the bacteria, but many people in developing countries are unable to boil their water because fuel is limited and costly, and other resources, like firewood, are scarce. Through her project, "Pasteurizing Water for the Third World," Rachael discovered a novel and quite promising method of pasteurizing, or sanitizing, undrinkable water. And she did it using a puddle.

"*As I researched the need for clean water,*" *wrote Rachael in her project summary,* "*I realized the importance of finding a safe, inexpensive, and practical way to provide clean water for developing countries. In my experiment, I questioned if water containing bacteria can be pasteurized practically and safely using a solar puddle.*"

Rachael got the idea for using a solar puddle from her research on the Internet. She liked this approach because the concept was so simple (a puddle heated

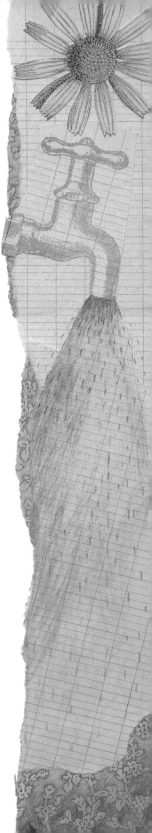

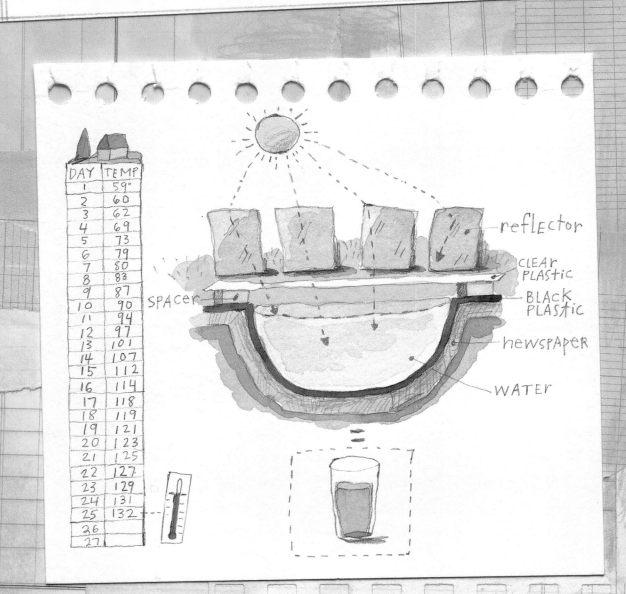

CURIOSITY Q

2000 — Tucson, Arizona — Rachael Charles

SOLAR WATER SANITIZATION

DAY	TEMP
1	59°
2	60
3	62
4	69
5	73
6	79
7	80
8	83
9	87
10	90
11	94
12	97
13	101
14	107
15	112
16	114
17	118
18	119
19	121
20	123
21	125
22	127
23	129
24	131
25	132
26	
27	

reflector

CLEAr PLASTIC

BLACK PLASTIC

SPACEr

hewsPAPEr

WATEr

by the sun), because it was inexpensive (between six and ten dollars), and because it was easy to construct (a few pieces of plastic, cardboard, and aluminum foil). But the question remained: would it work?

"I dug a small pit in our backyard and filled it with layers of newspaper insulation," explained Rachael. *"Then I put in a layer of black polyethylene plastic, then I put the pond water in and covered it with a sheet of clear polyethylene plastic, added spacers, and finally covered it with another sheet of clear plastic."*

Solar cookers, which work on the same basic principle as the solar puddle, are currently being tried in parts of Africa and Asia. While it was previously thought that the water had to reach 212 degrees Fahrenheit (water's boiling point), Rachael's puddle provided evidence that bacteria will be killed at lower—and easier-to-reach—temperatures.

After eight days of testing, it became apparent that she would need to raise the water temperature from its reading of 83 degrees. So she covered some cardboard sheets with aluminum foil and placed these homemade reflectors around the puddle. She recorded the temperatures for twenty-five days, and when the puddle reached 132 degrees, she decided to test her samples for bacteria.

"At the end of the experiment, tests were performed on both the original pond water and the water from the solar puddle to determine whether the solar puddle had effectively pasteurized the water," wrote Rachael. *"I found that the results were consistent with all three tests."*

For greater accuracy, she used three different testing methods—culturing samples in petri dishes, using a gram stain, and taking a water microbiology analysis. With the help of some professional testing labs, Rachael discovered that the majority of the harmful bacteria colonies had been eliminated; they had not survived the pasteurization process. The solar puddle had worked!

Rachael's project won her middle school science competition, and she advanced to the regional science fair. From there she went on to the Discovery Young Scientist Challenge, where she was named a finalist in the fall of 2000.

She plans to continue working on this project to find out whether it was the heat of the water or the ultraviolet rays of the sun that ultimately pasteurized the water. Because of its utter simplicity and doability, Rachael Charles's discovery that solar puddles can actually sanitize water may ultimately touch the lives of thousands—perhaps even save lives.

It is a discovery—like so many others—that is brimming with promise and possibility.

Your Turn

Now it's your turn to follow your own curiosity, your own desire to explore. And not just for answers to deep mysteries, but for things you simply didn't know before—things that might make you wonder . . .

Here are a few of the organizations, science competitions, and science fairs that encourage young people to explore and discover.

Roots & Shoots

This program of The Jane Goodall Institute emphasizes environmental and humanitarian programs for youth. The organization's goal is to inspire young people to participate actively in making the world a better place for animals, the environment, and our communities.

The Jane Goodall Institute
P.O. Box 14890
Silver Spring, MD 20911-4890
(301) 565-0086
Roots-Shoots@JaneGoodall.org

Discovery Young Scientist Challenge

Sponsored by Discovery Communications and Science Service, this science competition is for middle school students in grades 5–8. The competition gives awards for kids' knowledge of science and ability to communicate successfully about it.

Science Service
1719 N Street, NW
Washington, DC 20036
(202) 785-2255
www.school.discovery.com/sciencefaircentral/dysc

Bayer/NSF Award for Community Innovation

This competition, sponsored by the Bayer Corporation and the National Science Foundation, is for students in grades 6–8. The competition hopes to link kids to their communities through science and technology.

Bayer/NSF Award
105 Terry Drive, Suite 120
Newtown, PA 18940-3425
1 (800) 291-6020
www.bayernsfaward.com

Additional Web sites of interest

Solstice Project (sun-dagger calendar): www.solsticeproject.org
NASA (Sojourner): mars.jpl.nasa.gov/
The Field Museum (Sue the *T. rex*): www.fieldmuseum.org/Sue/
National Geographic: www.nationalgeographic.com
Discover magazine: www.discover.com
Scientific American Explorations magazine: www.explorations.org
Women Achievers: www.distinguishedwomen.com
Women in Science: www.suite101.com/links.cfm/women_in_science
Contributions of 20th-Century Women to Physics: www.physics.ucla.edu/

Sources

Interviews by the author:

Klara Bowman, Eli Penberthy, Erin Richardson, and Lindsey Watts, May 17, 2000; Rachael Charles, September 23, 2000; Wendy Freedman, June 5, 2000; Jane Goodall, April 6, 2000; Sue Hendrickson, May 26, 2000; June Moxon, November 24, 1999; Katie Murray, June 6, 2000; Vera Rubin, December 15, 1999; Denise Schmandt-Besserat, April 14, 2000; Donna Shirley, December 1, 1999; Anna Sofaer, January 19, 2000.

Clarke, Arthur C. *The Sands of Mars.* New York: Harcourt Brace, 1952. Reproduced by permission of Scovil Chichak Galen Literary Agency.

Leakey, Mary. *Disclosing the Past.* London: Rainbird Publishing Group, 1984, pp. 120, 121. Reproduced by permission of Penguin Books Ltd.

Shirley, Donna. *Managing Martians.* New York: Broadway Books, 1998. Reproduced by permission of Random House.

Quotations

"I think at a child's birth . . ." Eleanor Roosevelt. *Reader's Digest*, 1983; as quoted in *Quotations by Women*.

"Most new discoveries . . ." Susanne K. Langer. *Philosophy in a New Key*, 1942; as quoted in *Quotations by Women*.

"As human beings, we thrive . . ." Jean Fritz. *The Known and the Unknown: An Exploration into Non-fiction*, 1990; as quoted in *The Zena Sutherland Lectures 1983–1992*.

"If we would have new knowledge . . ." Susanne K. Langer. *Philosophy in a New Key*, 1942; as quoted in *The Beacon Book of Quotations by Women*, Rosalie Maggio.

"The power to question . . ." Indira Gandhi (1970). *Speeches and Writings*, 1975; as quoted in *The Beacon Book of Quotations by Women*, Rosalie Maggio.

Further Reading

Bertsch-McGrayne, Sharon. *Nobel Prize Women in Science (Their Lives, Struggles, and Momentous Discoveries)*. Seacaucus, N.J.: Carol Publishing Group, 1993.

Brown, Don. *Rare Treasure: Mary Anning and Her Remarkable Discoveries*. Boston: Houghton Mifflin, 1999. (For ages 4–8.)

Fagan, Brian M., editor. *Eyewitness to Discovery: First-Person Accounts of More than Fifty of the World's Greatest Archaeological Discoveries*. New York: Oxford University Press, 1996.

Goodall, Jane. *My Life with the Chimpanzees*. New York: Simon & Schuster, 1988.

Goodall, Jane. *With Love*. New York: North-South Books, 1998.

Pasachoff, Naomi. *Marie Curie and the Science of Radioactivity*. New York: Oxford University Press, 1996.

Poynter, Margaret. *The Leakeys: Uncovering the Origins of Humankind*. Chicago: Enslow, 1997.

Robinson, Fay, with the Science Team of The Field Museum. *A Dinosaur Named Sue: The Find of the Century*. New York: Scholastic, 1999.

Schmandt-Besserat, Denise. *The History of Counting*. New York: Morrow Jr. Books, 1999.

Sofaer, Anna, and Albert Ihde, producers. *The Sun Dagger*. Video. Bethesda, Md.: Atlas Video, 1983.

Sofaer, Anna, producer. *The Mystery of Chaco Canyon*. Video. Oley, Penn.: Bull Frog Films, 1999.

Stille, Darlene R. *Extraordinary Women Scientists*. Chicago: Children's Press, 1995.

Wunsch, Susi Trautmann. *The Adventures of Sojourner: The Mission to Mars That Thrilled the World*. New York: Mikaya Press, 1998.

Acknowledgments

The author wishes to thank the following for their contributions:

Sue Hendrickson; The Field Museum of Chicago; Vera Rubin; Donna Shirley; Rainbird Publishing Group, Penguin Books Ltd.; NASA; Anna Sofaer; Bull Frog Films; Denise Schmandt-Besserat; Morrow Jr. Books, HarperCollins; Jane Goodall; Mary Lewis; The Jane Goodall Institute; June Moxon; Wendy Freedman; Eli Penberthy; Erin Richardson; Klara Bowman; Lindsey Watts; Rachel Friedstein; Jessica Berenblum; Lauren Schulz; Raina Tripp; Karen Baker, Bayer/NSF; Katie Murray; Rachael Charles; Michelle Liden, Discovery Young Scientist Challenge; Dr. Hugh Torrens; Russell Galen, Scovil Chichak Galen Literary Agency; Broadway Books, Random House. My editor, Ann Rider, has my unending gratitude for her expert guidance.

Selected Timeline of Discoveries by Women

1300s   **ALESSANDRA GILIANI:** *how to trace blood vessels in cadavers*

1700s   **SOPHIE GERMAIN:** *mathematical theories to explain vibrations of elastic surfaces*

1700s   **SONYA KOVALEVSKI:** *partial differential equations and mathematical analysis of the shape of Saturn's rings*

1700s   **CAROLINE HERSCHEL:** *more than fourteen nebulae and eight comets*

1744   **ELIZA LUCAS PINCKNEY:** *indigo crops in the United States (South Carolina)*

1811   **MARY ANNING:** *ichthyosaurus; complete plesiosaur (1828)*

1847   **MARIA MITCHELL:** *a comet*

1854   **LATERINA SCARPELLINI:** *a comet*

1879   **MARIA DE SAUTUOLA:** *prehistoric cave art of Altamira, Spain*

1881   **WILLIAMINA PATON STEVENS FLEMING:** *222 variable stars; 10 novas*

1890s   **MARIE CURIE:** *radioactivity and radium*

1890s   **ANNA WESSEL WILLIAMS:** *effective antitoxin for diphtheria*

1890s   **DOROTHY REED (MENDENHALL):** *distinctive blood cells used to diagnose Hodgkin's disease, indicating that Hodgkin's is not a form of tuberculosis*

1901   **HARRIET ANN BOYD HAWES:** *a Minoan site at Gournia in Crete*

1902   **DR. FLORENCE SABIN:** *lymphatics*

1905   **NETTIE MARIA STEVENS:** *X and Y chromosomes*

1911   **ANNIE JUMP CANNON:** *300 new, variable stars*

1912   **HENRIETTA SWAN LEAVITT:** *Cepheid variables (stars that vary in brightness); nearly 2,000 variable stars*

1918   **EMMY NOETHER:** *mathematical formulas for Einstein's theory of relativity; abstract algebra (1921)*

1930 **CECILIA HELENA PAYNE-GAPOSCHKIN:** *chemical composition of stars; hydrogen and helium are the most abundant elements in stars, and therefore in the universe*

1930 **MARY CHUBB:** *statue of King Tut's wife*

1930 **MARIETTA BLAU:** *how to detect neutrons by using nuclear emulsions*

1930 **IDA EVA TACKE:** *the element 75-rhenium*

1934 **IRENE JOLIOT-CURIE:** *(contributed to) artificial radioactivity (Note: she is Marie Curie's daughter.)*

1934 **LISE MEITNER:** *nuclear fission, the splitting of atoms*

1936 **INGE LEHMANN:** *the earth's inner core*

1937 **MARGARET MORSE NICE:** *how birds nest (nesting behavior)*

1939 **GERTY CORI:** *the carbohydrate cycle*

1940 **RUTH PATRICK:** *that pollutants kill off most delicate species first, and therefore the health of an aquatic community indicates the degree of pollution*

1944 **DOROTHY CROWFOOT HODGKIN:** *the structure of penicillin, structure of vitamin B-12 (1956), structure of insulin (1969)*

1944 **HELEN BROOKE TAUSSIG:** *treatment for "blue babies"*

1944 **CHIEN-SHIUNG WU:** *the erroneousness of a fundamental law of physics: the "conservation of parity"*

1946 + **RITA LEVI-MONTALCINI:** *that tumors release an unknown growth factor; (isolated/identified) the nerve growth factor (NGF)*

1948 **TILLY EDINGER:** *that evolution does not occur in one straight line*

1948 **MARIA GOEPPERT MAYER:** *"magic numbers" (that certain atoms do not decay)*

1948 **ELIZABETH LEE HAZEN AND RACHEL BROWN:** *antifungal antibiotic*

1948 **PHYLLIS S. FREIER:** *evidence for presence of nuclei heavier than helium in cosmic radiation*

1950   ROSALYN YALOW: *radioimmunoassay (a technique that measures tiny quantities of biochemicals in the body)*

1950ᴧ   ROSALIND FRANKLIN: *(contributed to) the structure of DNA (Although two male scientists claimed credit and were awarded the Nobel Prize, most agree now the discovery was based on her work.)*

1951   BARBARA MCCLINTOCK: *"jumping genes" (genes move around and change the way traits come out in the next generation)*

1952   KATHLEEN KENYON: *ancient walls of Jericho; beginnings of farming and the birth of modern civilization*

1953   JUDITH GRAHAM POOL: *clotting process for hemophiliacs*

1956   DR. CHARLOTTE FRIEND: *virus that causes leukemia in mice*

1959   MARY LEAKEY: *fossil remains of ancient prehuman (1.75 million years old)*

1950ᴧ   EUGENIE CLARK: *sharks can be trained; eleven new species of fish/sea creatures*

1950ᴧ   GERTRUDE ELION: *leukemia and organ-transplant drug therapies*

1958   KATHERINE K. SANFORD: *how to clone a mammalian cell successfully (mouse)*

1960   JANE GOODALL: *that chimps use and make tools*

1962   RACHEL CARSON: *that pesticides can irrevocably damage the environment*

1967   JOCELYN BELL BURNELL: *pulsars*

1967   BETSY ANCKER-JOHNSON: *microwave emissions from an electron-hole plasma (microwave emissions without the presence of an external field)*

1967+   DIAN FOSSEY: *gorilla behavior patterns*

1970ᴧ+   JOAN WIFFEN: *dinosaur fossils in New Zealand*

1970ᴧ   VERA RUBIN: *dark matter*

1973   SANDRA MOORE FABER: *that colors and absorption-line strengths in spectra of elliptical galaxies vary with galaxy brightness*

1977 ANNA SOFAER: *sun-dagger calendar*

1983+ CAROLYN SHOEMAKER: *twenty-eight comets*

1987 K. ASLIHAN YENER: *ancient tin mine in Turkey; 5,000-year-old secret behind Bronze Age*

1989 JUNE MOXON: *a way to traverse the United States on a kinetic sculpture*

WANDA K. FARR: *the origin of cellulose*

1990^ CHRISTIANE NUSSLEIN-VOLHARD: *how a single cell becomes a complex creature*

1992 RENATA KALLOSH: *new phenomena in quantization of Kappa-symmetric gauge theories*

1994 ANN CYPHERS: *colossal head from Olmec culture*

1996 PAULA HAMMOND: *new technique for creating patterns and structures on surfaces*

1997 DONNA SHIRLEY: *small robots can be planetary explorers*

1998 WENDY FREEDMAN: *age of the universe*

FLOSSIE WONG-STAAL: *genes of the virus that causes AIDS*

1990^ JULIA CLARKE: *fossilized bones of unhatched (embryo) titanosaur*

1990^ MARGARET GALLAND KIVELSON: *(discovered and measured) the magnetic field of Ganymede (moon of Jupiter)*

2000 DR. MARTINA BERGER: *virus present in spinal cords of people who have ALS (Lou Gehrig's disease)*

2000 MAEVE LEAKEY: *3.5 million-year-old hominid skull (Note: she is Mary Leakey's daughter-in-law)*

Index

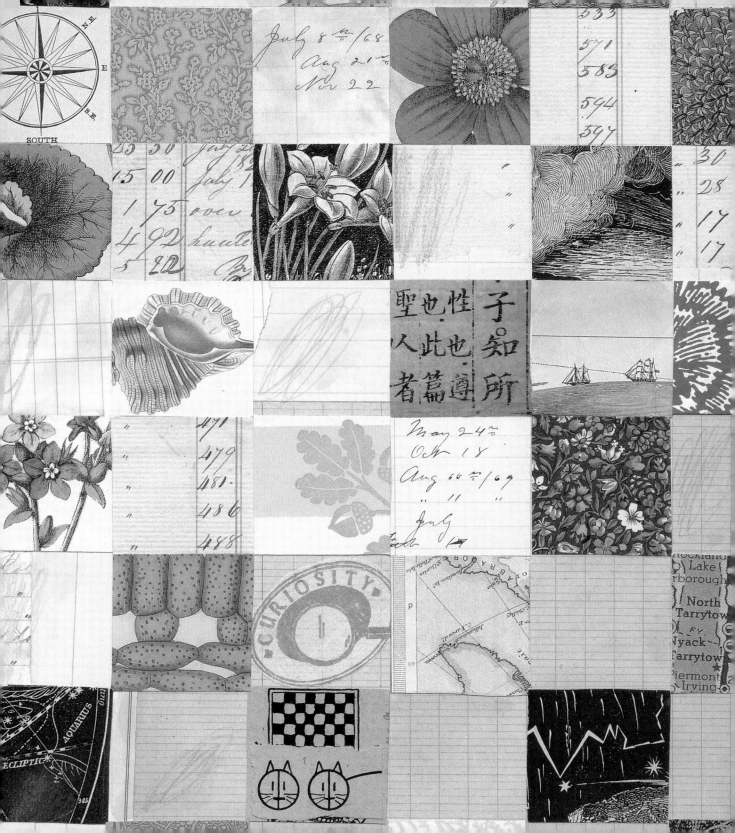